WHAT BOOKS PRESS

AN IMPRINT OF

THE GLASS TABLE

COLLECTIVE

LOS ANGELES

INSIDE THE UMBER IRIS

INSIDE THE UMBER IRIS

POEMS

ERIK MANUEL SOTO

WHAT
BOOKS
PRESS

LOS ANGELES

Library of Congress Cataloging-in-Publication Data

Names: Soto, Erik Manuel, 1993- author
Title: Inside the umber iris : poems / Erik Manuel Soto.
Description: Los Angeles : What Books Press, 2025. | Summary: "Inside the
    Umber Iris is a collection of poems that traverses the realms of the
    subconscious and mythology. A lyrically surrealist style, with themes of
    generational trauma and folkloric genealogy, creates an odyssey with
    high emotional stakes. Pain and passion are continuously guiding each
    stanza, each line"-- Provided by publisher.
Identifiers: LCCN 2025030370 | ISBN 9798990014985 paperback
Subjects: LCGFT: Poetry
Classification: LCC PS3619.O8635 I57 2025
LC record available at https://lccn.loc.gov/2025030370

Cover art: Gronk, *Untitled*, mixed media on paper, 2024
Book design by ash good, www.ashgood.com

What Books Press
363 South Topanga Canyon Boulevard
Topanga, CA 90290

WHATBOOKSPRESS.COM

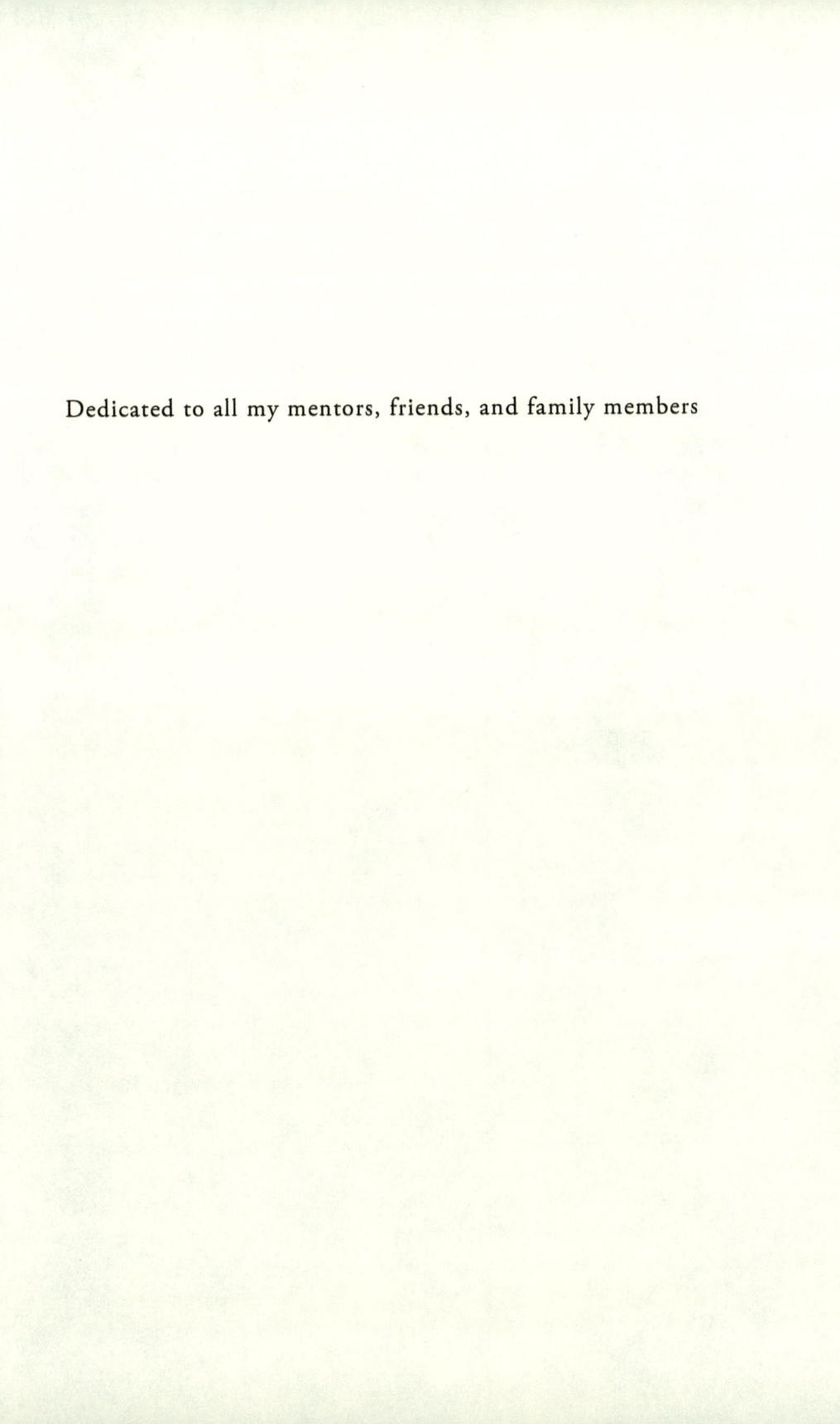

Dedicated to all my mentors, friends, and family members

CONTENTS

Isn't it often in our most intimate relations
that we come to realize that our identity,
all identity, is combinatory?

—Forrest Gander

PART I

COME AS YOU ARE,

        cursed song

tearing snails out

        from bellflower petals,

invisible to the loitering

        sun shower.

Quetzalcóatl completely coils

        into jade crystallization

and butterflies wear

        fading indigo gradience

on their wings to camouflage

        from starved lambs.

All dark apple cores fear

        your sombering grass.

Song, hold onto my hand

        when you discover

the murder of innocent

        wavering wheat fields

came from your polluting chorus.

INDAPARAPEO, MICHOACAN II

On the thorny cactus,
the skin of a rattlesnake.

Under a broken brick,
a scorpion's black entrails.

In the lonely sidewalk,
a mute beggar desires

a waning moon to fall
with wounded wild dogs.

Thin fog and orange street lights
fight with lunging umbras,

but I didn't come here to watch
a horizon of clouded blood.

I came here to escape blood
stained carpets and the memory

of mother begging for mercy.
I came here to lose myself

in the feathers of spotted owls
becoming the small underbellies

of birthed fawns becoming white
jasmine corsages becoming

passing star constellations.
I came here to escape,

but now I stand in front
of a sleeping slaughterhouse

smelling pig malodor.

I DREAMED OF TOUCHING

My mother's swollen cheek

and comforting her shaking hands

with a votive burning a fat flame

but it became the red muleta

craving the murder of her bull

by having the bullfighter

strike pink banderillas

on his nape.

Ole, Ole, Ole,

let the dead bull's tongue

taste the pissed dirt.

BEING A POET IN THE BIGGEST LITTLE CITY

is waiting for stars to fall

and become mosaic

trail paths where a lead-pierced duck

flails from the mouth

of an obeying dog.

Most hours however

are neon lit cheekbones

of addicts abandoning sleep

in the long-scabbed streets shouting

for mercy, or in madness —

it's hard to tell really

when pomegranates are thrown

out of hotel windows

and your eyes tell you

glowing cigarettes in mouths passing

are suns being swallowed by Tezcatlipoca

and spat back out as salt.

Somewhere in the city

there is a canyon

of rotting limes bared

in the scar of a bartender's wrist.

Her rusting ring carrying

a turquoise gem resurrected

from the high-desert grounds.

Most hours are lost

to constant vertigo

the bruising kaleidoscopic blur

in underground rave clubs

the cold grit of bathroom sinks

believing blow is holy

if not, it's at least the moment

before the bull charges

towards the bullfighter.

ALL THICK-THORNED ROSES CHASED ME

into the mouth of a jaguar

    until my heart became a dying red Moon.

        Then Venus dropped me on hard dirt

            discovered moths wear oil-slick-halos

                to distract away from fruit corpses.

                    Then I saw my hands, bruised blue,

                        choking a bronze bull

                            but as the light of fireflies

                                got closer, it was my father

                            flailing.

IF THE OBSIDIAN BOTTLE COULD TALK

You might find out your father

was once velvet-hearted

in the prairie where the lure

of milkweeds taught him to love

the sun-starved berries,

the gaunt goats with severed horns.

If the obsidian bottle could talk,

it would tell you, your father touched

emerald and became feathered—

glided above cenotes

in search of the sweet pulp

Yucatec opuntias guard.

If the obsidian bottle could talk,

you would know, your father's wings

were wounded by his father

with cigarette butts

and shards of wine bottles.

Father knows grasshoppers gnaw

on ambered skies,

he has seen eagles emerge out

the underbelly of cows,

and has witnessed his father

turn his mother's eye sockets

into aster petals.

THE TARANTULAS ARE SLEEPING

And I, in this wandering dawn

hang on the cold shoulders of a rhinoceros.

Look, I don't remember how I got here

but from this view of the sidewalk

the few moving cars are headless gazelles leaping.

I know I have a problem

but the wooly weeds on cracked cement are calling

so are the mothless lamps

and the fire ants I kill with my thumbs.

Look, I don't remember how I got here

maybe it was the dented San Francisco sand

or the legless gray gull starving.

All I remember was mom left a voicemail

telling me she was threatened to a death.

BREATHING THROUGH THE WOUND

"Ojo por ojo, diente por diente"

I want to own the white fangs

wolves strike on throats

bisons witness in their eyes

to set fields of honeysuckle ablaze.

Or maybe I crave to watch

the coral reefs slowly suffocate

in oiled oceans, despite conch shell

pearls offering the Moon

as a surrendering tribute.

It's all a denunciation to the rivers

that see daffodils grow

near the sun-absent mountains

when I'm sitting, ear-attached-to-wall,

as my mother is getting purple-eyed.

I want the trickling rain drops

on windows to be fire striking Earth

for the silence after I ask:

why is my mother purple-eyed?

TWILIGHT IS DROWNING

and there is a spoiled mango

in my room

preaching fatalism

with a mouth formed of ants.

Tell me again

why begging the dreamscape

for a pitch-dark-sleep

isn't the same as praying?

BLURRY-EYED,

in the blue murk
of jazz club
where center stage
is decorated with calico rug,
I fail to find God
in the trombone's moving tongue
or the golden wave of saxophone solo.
The acoustic séance of crowd
invokes shadows
the shape of reaper-robes.
Tonight, the corner of the bar
is the black opulent corpse
of a crow. No.
It's the smooth underbelly of a bull
murdered for its glorious ear.
I can't see God in the lustrous lit hallway
leading to white
powdered bathroom sinks
but I do see the rotting gut
of an ostrich devoured
by spotless hyenas
laughing with the cadence
of a catholic hymn.

SÉANCE UNDER A LUNAR ECLIPSE

Oh Tezcatlipoca, I offer you my silent clavicle
    and the rib where the blind iguana
        bites for not dreaming.
        Escape the depths your summit
    whether it be the volcano
layered with flattened obsidian
    that deceives the dark ceilings of caverns
        with a starry night's glisten
        or the green feathered
    imprisonment of heaven
where alms are no longer human organs
    only votives opaque with old
        mourning at your mercy.
Oh nahual of a jaguar, I admit
    there was no catholic God
        when the kernel of red maize
        sprouted plagued molars
    and the marble sculpted Christ,
that appeared, stared while husk became
    lips pining over a broken heart.
Oh Tezcatlipoca, I offer you my quiet collarbone
    for a death by serpent venom
        in the field where bees relieve
        lilies from the weight of their nectar.

I TRIED TO MEND MY HEART

with the cold lace

of snow slopes

and the scent of white

Jeffrey pines

but the perishing clouds

called my name

and showed me a coyote

carcass under a pocket

of an opening sky.

Now I want to feel

the troubling eye

of horned owls

that haunt me

when sadist hyacinths

fantasize about needle-prodded

caterpillars during dusk.

ONLY IDIOTS GET LOST IN DREAMS

and yet, you are here again, in the cusp of desert realm playing
poker with skull-faced pachucos and gambling the head of a
xoloitzcuintli. You're holding a flush of tarot cards, all with the
image of a fallen son being ripped apart by gathering vultures.
The lonely petunia next to you blossoms a black hole in its pistil,
swallowing you into a landscape of red gorges. There, burnt sheep
are pushing Romans into pits of burning phosphorus but a raft
of gray pelicans saves you. They take you back into a poker game,
but this time a pair of eye-filled wings watches.

II

Now sirens hold me hostage. How the sun sours when bright

blue lights blur the pupils. Should I become a magpie and fly

behind the billboard where pigeons are plum-hearted? Or should

I metamorphosize into a silver cocoon? I'll hide until cops retreat,

and then I'll hatch as an owl-eyed butterfly to seek asylum in a

forest filled with cypress trees.

FOLKLORIC DISSONANCE

Even the crows in your teeth know
you've abandoned the dahlias
blossoming around the stones
of Teotihuacan. I tell you sincerely
you are a son lost in the alleys
of the insomniacs addicted to cocaine,
moth tattoos, and nights when the Moon
swallows all the staring irises.

Child, you are lost, not in a dream
but in the orifice of a Montana sky
where buffalos multiply despite
car-torn-tar wandering into their bellies.
You are lost to the nebulas found
in red beryls and the melancholic breeze
passing through bare sagebrushes.

Son, you are lost, but childhood opuntias
wait for your return. Frida's orange madness
waits for your return. The folkloric suit
your father wore waits for you
to dance — a quetzal bird
fluttering over a glistening cenote.

IN EVERY SUN-KISSED DREAM

the pink epiphyllum tucked

in Frida's hair asks:

Does your heart still ache?

Yes, Frida, it hurts to be honey.

Between skin and nail

there are daisies with golden yolks

searching for soil

the color of concave olives.

Even if the assemblage of all dying

grapes were to find solace

in emerald-bottled glasses,

I'd still see the skulls of monkeys

solarized on hooks tethered

to the corner of eroding bricks.

Frida, it hurts to be honey,

under a waning morning

I wander without a compass.

For the purple cauliflowers are misleading

and the spotted orchids

speak of nothing other than

the time my heart desired a kiss

from lips soft as orange petals.

It hurts to be honey.

The prismatic shapes

stitched on your shawl

are impatient-drawn coffins

masquerading as empty honeycombs.

And I know each ditch is a mouth

waiting to consume me.

PART II

FRAGMENTED DREAMS

.

.

.

.

.

.

.

In the garden where wolves come to die,

where the imprinted leaves on stones wait

to possess the bodies of fallen pinecones

and where God visits, disguised as a snake,

to supervise resurrecting antlers,

Father appears in the collecting burning-wisps

of wasp hives —

the ethereal twister, whispering

closely to my earlobe:

¿Dónde estabas cuándo sepultaron a tu tío?

.

.

．

．

．

The desert calls my name,

lure of a blue skyline

when the Moon is salient

despite sunlight illuminating

my bronze irises.

Sometimes saguaros send love letters

through the claws of golden eagles.

Stamped with white petals,

they write: *Comeback! Comeback!*

Comeback, and visit grandpa's ashes!

．

．

．

．

．

.

.

No, the bull's heart doesn't want

a bouquet of marigolds on its altar,

it wants you, as a shard of obsidian

dagger, to pierce it in its center

so it can clasp you down beneath

the Jupiters that have collapsed,

beneath the scorpion scales

fallen prey to gnomes that guard

the polygonal bleeding jaspers.

There, in that underworld,

Xolotls stand holding spears decorated

with gorilla skulls

and father is waiting,

inside a conch shell without lips

¿Por qué te has tardado tanto en salvarme?

.

.

.

．

You've returned, as ash on the cracks of brick walls,

        as ash on the lamp bulb charming lost moths,

        as ash on the rim of beer cans

with endless pits,

        where only monarchs and suns

          rise out of their mouths

and become crystal sediments

        swept by a southern breeze.

          Grandfather, you've returned as ash,

alarmingly soft on the concrete flooring

        belonging to crickets with scissored torsos,

        the insects that cry

when soil loses its fertility.

        Grandfather, you've returned

          but why are you here?

why are you here as ash?

        why are you here, resting silently,

          on my heart-shaped hooves?

．

.

.

.

.

.

.

How beautiful is it to drift through the dawning

        sea urchins orchestrating séances

        in hunger for resurrection, uncle?

Are cold-flecked corpses searching to kiss rosemaries

        on the field of dehydrated pear-peels?

        Sorry, uncle —sadly, our patrimony

is either small talk or silence.

        What I want to ask is

        Do you forgive me for not being there?

.

.

.

.

Put my heart on the scale

that has sent the howling

mornings into cow pupils

the maggots consume

and weight it in comparison

to the silver-skinned apple

harvested from the tree

my ancestors were hung

and if the balance tips

against my favor

tell my father he never had a son.

Tell him I was just a shadow

of sold sunflowers he kept

until dried, then fed

to the blue horses

passing through the collar bone

of Indaparapeo.

.

.

.

.

.

.

I dreamt my suicide note

was scrawled all over

Diego Rivera's *Detroit Industry*

.

.

.

.

.

.

.

.

THE ONE WHO LEAVES
CLEANSES THE WORLD

With a heart that's seen

riotous dreams live

beyond the confines

of a curving skull

I think all violet-headed weeds

know a swollen night

that coping by gnawing

on bathroom sinks

isn't going to end

the goat's horns from piercing

the ribcage repeatedly

or that making peace

with a burning chalice

only leads to scorpions

stinging the naked body.

Oh, what a torment!

Oh, what a torment!

Pienso, el que parte

limpia el mundo   - Omar Caceres

      .

               .

               .

               .

               .

               .

               .

               .

               .

               .

Let the navel of peyotes sever

    from my veins. I am tired of being

        a child helplessly watching caterpillars

           manducate cempasuchiles

                under the hour when the underbelly

                of a Quetzal expands into a horizon line.

        I am tired of seeing

        my mother beaten in dreams,

    or sitting on concrete stairs,

crying, begging for the sun-touched

    opulence found in dew droplets,

        to end the long violent night.

           Let the ox tails in my mother's hair

                choke me dead. Let the cicatrized Moons

                found in my mother's scleras

           collide into a field of stunted trees

        where mossed copper accompanies me.

        Let the jaguar leaping out

my mother's mouth

    kill me.

PART III

MY MAGNUM OPUS

I will write my Magnum Opus
                            and watch a golden eagle
hunt during the hour of mice.
                            One day the heartless sun will devour
the scales of crocodiles
                            swallow tethered spiderwebs
where moths surrender white wings.
                            I'll listen to the lyric lurk
where thin feet meet hot sand
                            where tequila-drunk eyes look at
cacti and hear a verse or muse
                            whisper *limn me*
like a rorschach canvas.
                            I will write my magnum opus,
despite, the dusk-glow glazing
                            the irises of starving coyotes.
The wilting roses might drown
                            in the piss of drunks
and the crescent skyline
                            will wait for death dressed in lavender.

DUSK WAS A SCARLET TONGUE

in my ear, warning me

of the boar carcasses

when I returned from the cemetery

of half-sliced papayas.

There, I showed caterpillars

how to become Moon-cocooned

before carbon-taloned owls pierced

their fat napes.

There, only earwigs forgot

to avoid chiseled gravestones

that wept when lilies didn't gift

them their soft touch.

There, the tripe of a vulture was the string

on Mictlantecuhtli's necklace

with parrot feathers as emerald garnets,

a glistening of grasshopper wings,

Mictlantecuhtli said:

Konetl, mitsalone a,

iuan mitsalone mikis.

 kenih tlauilli tlamatoka

inon kamiltiixpolomeh

mitsmochintin uil itta ka mikistli

Son, alone you come here,

and alone you will die.

When sunrise touches

those umber eyes,

all you will see is death.

ALL THE DYING SUNFLOWERS

Before a slug eats a slug out on the wet pathway, and before fake goblets shatter by the hands of a deranged drunk, hold me softly under these opaque neon signs. It's okay if you don't love me. I know I'm crazy for speaking of the lurking goblins, of the Dadaist holding a broken hourglass, of the antelope with arms as antlers. I know I'm crazy. This morning I gazed at the flying geyser and it became the head of Quetzalcóatl telling me I will die in Granada with a violent rainstorm. It's okay if you don't love me, but in dreams, I keep watching fields of sunflowers burn, I keep hearing rioting winds whistle in ache, and right now, the collapsed addict smells of a familiar death. So please, before the howling sirens arrive, hold me softly under these opaque neon signs.

PREVENTING THE SON FROM FRACTURING

You don't. Even if you were to sacrifice

a flying fox during the birth of a solar eclipse,

the son would still lose himself

to the wildflowers plucked

by the longing of passing fingers.

Let the son break, for the ox snouts

he sees in every shattered church

window spurt crystalized feathers

from the misery moths find

in the yellow hours.

Let the son break, so he can touch

the antlers shedding

the furs of all the hung coati heads

and have them become berries

blossoming out the stems of spikenards.

Let him break, if there's no stopping

mallards from drowning in polluted ponds,

if there's no stopping

falling aeroiths from ending Earth,

then let him break

into the crepuscular fragments

where he can turn purple badges

into stone amethysts.

AMBULANCE

Soft-brained
      and sallow-skinned,
            I lie on a white stretcher.
                  The sting of IV syringe
spreads throughout
      my forearm.

                              Can you hear me, son?

I hear God's
      silence.
            This is how I know
            he's a man.
How many times
      under the quiet
            of waxing Moons,
                  have I held rosaries
praying for his love?
      A sign from him,
            whether it be
                  a whisper
a breeze
      or the illusion
            of holy light
                  could have tamed
my fear of falling
      into my father's
            addictions.

                          Where does it hurt the most?

Sometimes I think
  an odyssey isn't
   an odyssey
    unless pain is involved.
Like how a man
  isn't a man
   unless his hands
    are calloused and scarred.

This is how I know
  God is a man.
   He only saved his son
    after he saw
the holes in his palms.

    Is there anyone we should contact?

I could slice
  open the insides
   of a sheep
    set up altars
decorated with marigolds
  or self-inflict
   starvation as a sign
    of penance
and God would still ignore
  my calling
   for a cosmic
    relief.

How many more silences
do I have to endure
for God to consider me
a man
worth saving?

NO USE CRYING

when walls wear descending twin shadows
the shape of snake tongues.

There is no use in covering the ears
those murmurs bleed through finger-gaps

becoming anger-stricken utterings
 and creating cacophony

against the sound of a swigging whiskey bottle.
Sleepless and stiffened-up,

this is the hour where crepuscular light
is the marauding wildflower

blooming hands that strike the cheek,
legs that kick the side,

a longhorn's corpse that haunts
the witnessing eye.

OH MADRE, NO LLORES

Yo sé que he caído en las profundidades del alcoholismo. Salir
será perderme en un laberinto, pero me acompaña el duende
enamorado con rosas amarillas. Me cuidan los xoloitzcuintles
negros de Moctezuma, y persigo una luna tierna. Madre, no estes
triste. Esta distancia tal vez será una desolación, pero el océano
pacifico canta sonoramente, y los saguaros guiando, son de un
verde esmeralda. Caer en soledad no es un castigo, es aprender a
ser un colibrí.

OH MOTHER, DON'T CRY

I know I have fallen into the depths of alcoholism. To come out is to get lost in a labyrinth, but I am accompanied by the goblin in love with yellow roses. I am guarded by Montezuma's black xoloitzcuintle, and I chase a tender Moon. Mother don't be sad. This distance may be bleak, but the Pacific Ocean sings sonorously, and the guiding saguaros are an emerald green. Falling into solitude is not a punishment, it is learning how to be a hummingbird.

OH MOTHER, DON'T CRY

The goblin turned out to be a dog-gaze thief and only left smeared whorls on the neck of the perished xoloitzcuintle. Yes, mother, this means the ocean fell mute, abandoning me with hands that ripped cacti pads, thinking they were tequila-swollen agave leaves, for my liquor longing lips to moisten. Every insignificant gleam was an imitation of a streetlight reflected on whiskey glass, luring me to blindly step on the slugs without direction. On the salt stuck inside salvia droplets left by a fleeing opossum. I wandered in front of a Mictlantecuhtli altar. No mother, there is no escape insight, but please don't cry. Perhaps I can ask Mictlantecuhtli for help.

OH MOTHER, DON'T CRY

Mother, I can't escape this labyrinth of lamb hooves formed into flagstones leading to ends where talons dance with ivy bushes. I find myself caught in the chambering tumbleweed. Take this letter as a rendering to the moss that grows in the hollowed-eye socket of an oak trunk, where fallen Moons dissolve into granite-dust. Mother, don't cry, I know mothers should never hear of their child's imprisonment, but when the mouth of Mictlantecuhtli captures you, mother, you become an eagle without wings.

WITHOUT SLEEP

In this weeping morning
the tender protest of breeze
strikes the yellow teeth
of brown bears
and the resurrected monarchs
chase wild dogs.
If the silver clouds fall
inside mason jars
know that nightmares eat
the petals of dandelions.
If fruit flies soar out
the folds of palms
when the wandering donkey
licks dirty snow
know that nightmares ingest
granite directly out of the soft Earth.
And if the farthest cemetery hosts
a pond of floating green coins
when sallow grass grows salt
know that a starved nightmare is waiting
for the eyelids to close.

THE BEGINNING OF DETACHMENT

Quiet corner-coiled boy, eyes in slow drift-fall.

Forget the hour marking mother with purple badges.

Forget the sight of father fist-clenched

drunk-faced falling on an olive couch.

Crepuscular light. Imagine shadows are antlers.

Your hands, hooves, holding hibiscus.

Wipe those trailing tears.

Pretend your cheeks are covered with glittering copper.

Otherwise, dream, boy, dream.

CÚRATE CON LOS RAYOS DEL SOL

After María Sabina

Cúrate con los rayos del sol
or if you can't, drink coffee.
See the orange hibiscuses
cascading out of the yolks
of your trembling fingers.
They might become monarchs
symbolizing a changing landscape.
A seed blossoming despite
a turbulent Saturn storm.

Cúrate con el río que sonríe
when a soft silvering spring
gifts caterpillars wings
for surviving the flooding rain.
For somehow, watching spiders
drown and still choosing
to climb slanting trees.

Cúrate aunque pienses

                        en suicidio.

The porcelain mug

                        you are holding

is only slightly

                        chipped.

SIN ESPERANZA

Después de Frida Kahlo

Beneath the eyeless light of Sun
the Moon an adjacent witness
I lie naked and alone among
the mountainous range of umber granite.

Tucked in covers the color of sugar skulls
I see my skull purge out of my lips
with the entrails of animals
I have slaughtered and consumed
back when my cobalt-blue wallson
still inspired me to paint.

There on the splintered easel
I see my heart glazed with pig's blood
slowly deflating into its last muscle spasms.
I tell you I stopped believing in stars.

Planets have fallen out of the sky
and stitched themselves onto my bed
but I no longer believe I was born
inside the cradle of the Moon.

ABUELITO, I HAVE DREAMED
OF YOU SO MUCH

that I've become familiar with the dandelion lure
gusting through the slug-starved meadow
where you stand, with cupped palms,
holding my heart for the stars to kiss.

Is there time to reach your shrinking body today?

Sadly, even in dream-state mice gnaw
mossing antlers, a fleeing salamander bleeds
out its missing tail, and the hair on your head
falls like a cloud without wings.

Can I reach your shrinking body today?

Sadly, bladed grass slits my legs
as I am chased by a wandering swarm
of wasps. And in our verdant distance,
I watch you slowly become umber dust.

LOST IN THE HOUR OF RED CHAOS

Oh, how I fear you red.
You are the droplets falling

down my eyes
   when prickly pears rot

      with red umbilical cords
         and ruby-winged dragonflies glide

         out of crystal ambers.
            Jupiter's red spot swallows

               phosphorus sand and red ribbons
               rope the throats of dahlias.

               Oh, how I fear you red.
            Dawns are bleeding skies

            surrendering sugar grains
         to the lips of the insatiable dadaists.

      There the Sonoran dunes are electric red
   there thunder sets the palms
   of artists aflame.

Oh, how I fear you red.
You come out at night

dripping out of my mother's
mouth, painting trails

of red rorschach.
Your canvas, a whiskey
smelling carpet.

PALABRAS ENCONTRADAS
EN LA BOCA DE MI PADRE

"Look, son, things got out of control. I never meant to hurt your

mother. Each alcoholic night, I was swallowed in the crater of a

panther's mouth and reborn as a mystic grape with a shattered

reflection. Mornings were a kaleidoscopic confusion wolf claws

find with sand, only to figure I was purple causing. Only to figure

your umber eyes were falling hollow. Son, I swore I wouldn't

repeat the violence I saw my mother take, yet we are here. Tell me

do you hate me?

It's okay if you do."

FIELD OF SUGARCANES

A machete severs the head of a toad

       that leapt without a clouded heart,

or with the hope of finding

       a faceless mandolin to hide.

The nasturtiums cry

       for the tender wind

that saw nothing was fluttering

       after it gave its cupped hands

to the butterfly growing grass

       out of its abdomen.

It's all a snake's skull, here.

       Buried fangs to fossils,

diseased internodes to plague roots.

I mourn the leopard cub killed

    by the blade. Yes, I mourn

the leopard cub sacrificed for a crop

    to produce nothing but worms.

NIGHTS PACING BY

blur into

sleepwalking street-dogs

into the faint metronome

of inhaling beggars

or pigeons struggling

with plastic

as nooses.

Dissociative spiraling

is an orange peel

cars run over

until it becomes muck

the cornered storm draining

refuses to swallow.

GO HOME

To hear the bullfrogs sing
in the drying river
where weeping willows
wait for blue larks to return.

There is no lily growing out
the eye socket of a dead atheos,
no cornucopia filled with rotten grapes,
goat intestine spiraling throughout twined frame.

Go home, and see the distance cigarette glow
gull in fireflies before the Moon
wakes black widows out of their hollowed logs.

The melting compasses pointing toward
a fingerless greek painter are not there
nor is the merciless scythe
still dripping with the blood of a muse.

Run home, to avoid the labyrinth
where cymbals and pomegranates hide
from the wooden lyre for suffocating
the throat of a white horse with its strings.

Back home, the harvested honey waits,

and the overwintering monarchs

roost in the Monterey cypresses

YERBA BUENA

Grandmother, in what gray coated cloud does your heart rest?

Sometimes I think I hear your voice rustle from the shoulders

of a blue-tailed lizard, or perhaps, in the swaying frail tips of

sagebrush surviving summer. In this departing hour, a silver

horizon falls beneath my feet and I wish I'd become a fading

lunar eclipse. Perhaps then, I'd stop dreaming of black scorpions

crawling out of the mouths of French philosophers. Perhaps

then, the dream where rain drizzles sharp pineapple rinds,

and redwood trees wear a thousand bovine eyes, would end.

Grandmother, resurrect your spirit-healing hands and cure me

by smearing rubbing alcohol and spearmint leaves on my skin. I

want to know I am still your child and ask it so because I want

the Morelia marigolds to know. I want the mossy stone blocks of

Tzintzuntzan to know. I want Mictlantecuhtli and Tezcatlipoca

to know. Today, I thought I heard your voice blow in from a

southern current and billow into idyllic winds heading toward

the sun, but it was a green-winged hummingbird fluttering above.

YERBA BUENA

Abuelita, ¿en qué esmalte gris de nube descansa tu corazón? A veces creo oír tu voz susurrar desde los hombros de un lagarto de cola azul, o tal vez en las frágiles puntas oscilantes de la artemisa que sobrevive el verano. En esta hora de partida, cae un horizonte plateado bajo mis pies y deseo ser un eclipse solar que se desvanece. Quizás entonces, dejaría de soñar con escorpiones negros saliendo de la boca de los filósofos franceses. Quizás entonces, terminaría el sueño donde la lluvia rocía cáscaras afiladas de piña y las secuoyas lucen mil ojos bovinos. Abuela, resucita tus manos sanadoras y cúrame untando alcohol y hierba buena sobre mi piel. Quiero saber que sigo siendo tu hijo y te lo pido porque quiero que las maravillas de Morelia lo sepan. Quiero que los bloques de piedra musgosas de Tzintzuntzan lo sepan. Quiero que Mictlantecuhtli y Tezcatlipoca lo sepan. Hoy, creí escuchar tu voz soplar desde los vientos del sur y separarse en una corriente ascendente que se dirigía hacia el sol, pero era un colibrí de alas verdes que revoloteaba sobre mí.

FOR THE ROMANTIC WOLF

Jasmine rivers crossed are blood.

Your demise isn't falling among

milk petals, no, your dying is undiscovered

sedimentary obsidian, suffocating

under bear claws, the concave hunger

of rats, a Leo sun staining deer ribs

on dry dirt. Jasmine rivers crossed

are blood, and so are the wounded roses

you followed into the cavern where

eyes are the lampposts of secret lovers

and you are a secret lover, only stood-up,

wishing the Jasmine rivers you crossed were your blood.

LOVE POEM

After Lorca's "To Find a Kiss of Yours"

Today, you stare at me

with brown-eyed gaze

tethering the light of twilight

like violet hitches

onto the lens of a kaleidoscope.

Under the gypsy-hot Moon

your hair glints

silvery black strands

of sculpted planetary elegance

and all I can think is

what would I give?

To see sunrise slip

through the gaps

of window blinds

and wake you out

of thick cheetah

printed bed sheets.

To watch you make your dress

dance to the rhythm

of dandelions and bumblebees

in the plain grassy terrain

of wine country.

To hear you whisper my name

in the back aisle

of a small library

while you show me a Spanish copy

of *Cien años de soledad.*

To feel you grasp

my forearm when riding

the green swirling rails

of Medusa's roller coaster,

what would I give?

I'd give the rain

and rainbow in the shapes

of wandering garnets

that become the hearts of Saguaros.

Awnings of blue beryls

forged from the sediments

of May's morning skyline.

I'd give the bronze amber

of my irises only found

in the chambered

treasures of Mesoamerica

and the blood of my Mexica

ancestors turned into

a carnelian bracelet.

To see you stare at me

with brown-eyed gaze

what would I give?

I'd surrender my body

to an apocalyptic Earth.

VALS POÉTICO

Mi corazón se convirtió
en la forma de una biznaga,
con mil espinas,
cuando la pendiente de nieve
rindió su costilla izquierda
para que exista las artemisas
ingratas junto a licorerías.

Algunos gansos se comieron
sus propios ojos.
Algunos petirrojos amputaron
sus propias garras.
Aun así, la luna daría nació
y se reío cuando descubrió
que el gato atropellado,
que manchaba la acera blanca,
tomó la forma de mi corazón.

VALS POÉTICO

My heart became the shape
of a barrel cactus,
wearing a thousand thorns,
when the snow slope surrendered
it's left rib for the ungrateful
sagebrushes to exist
next to liquor stores.

Some geese ate their own eyes.
Some robins amputated
their own claws.
Still, the daily Moon birthed
and laughed when it discovered
cat roadkill staining
the white sidewalk
took the shape of my heart.

IF YOU'RE READING THIS,

don't you worry about me.

I negotiated with the yellowing skyfall

to become the daily shadow

of a tree engraved

with the initials of temporary lovers.

I will be passing wind hugging

you in your dreams,

the one kissing Moon craters for you.

Don't you worry about me,

in angel-beat-glory,

I was born within marigolds

cradled by omens, or Andromeda,

some cosmic delirium

feeling empathetic towards the raw of red.

Please, don't you worry about me,

if anything just know

now I am a hummingbird.

ACKNOWLEDGMENTS

My eternal gratitude to the following people who helped me grow as a poet and as a person during the time leading up to this poetry collection:

Gillian Conoley, Kathleen Winter, Jared Stanley, Gailmarie Pahmeier, Steven Gehrke, Daniel Enrique Perez, Guadalupe Escobar, Stefan Kiesbye, Anne Goldman, Elliot Coyle, Courtney Cliften, Caryn Dreibelbis, Nicholas Pulito, Nicolette Clark, Brooke Wrisley, Helen Gainy, Hannah Rouley, Breanne Cassells, David Ramirez, Jesus Ramirez, Steve Djekou, Bryanna Haynes, Efrain Tena, and of course, my family members.

A special thanks to these magazines & journals for publishing the following poems:

Volt: "Folkloric Dissonance," "For the Romantic Wolves," "All thick-thorned roses chased me"

The Nevada Poetry Project: "Being a Poet in the Biggest Little City"

The Nelligan Review: "Yerba Buena"

River and South Review: "Ambulance"

Huizache: "All the Dying Sunflowers"

The Dewdrop: "Seance Under a Lunar Eclipse"

Clackamas Literary Review: "The Beginning of Detachment"

 ERIK MANUEL SOTO is a Mexican-American writer from California. His poems have appeared in *Volt 27*, *the Nelligan*, *River and South Review*, *Huizache* and *Sonora Review*. Winner of the inaugural Gronk Nicandro first book prize for poetry, Erik debuts his full length poetry collection, *Inside the Umber Iris*. He is currently bouncing around the West Coast.

WHAT BOOKS PRESS

AN IMPRINT OF

THE GLASS TABLE

COLLECTIVE

LOS ANGELES

WHAT BOOKS feature cover art by Los Angeles painter, printmaker, muralist, and theater and performance artist GRONK. A founding member of ASCO, Gronk collaborates with the LA and Santa Fe Operas and the Kronos Quartet. His work is found in the Corcoran, Smithsonian, LACMA, and Riverside Art Museum's Cheech Marin collection.

As a small, independent press, we urge our readers to support independent publishers and booksellers. This is easily done by visiting our website, WhatBooksPress.com, where you can purchase books directly from us or from Bookshop.org

2025

Inside the Umber Iris
ERIK MANUEL SOTO
WINNER OF THE GRONK
NICANDRO FIRST BOOK PRIZE
POEMS

Persistence of Singing Woods
JOHN COLBURN
STORIES

River of Angels
STEPHEN COOPER
STORIES

Jukebox
PATTY SEYBURN
POEMS

zirconium ash
JIMMY VEGA
POEMS

It Wasn't Always Like This
JAN WESLEY
POEMS

2024

The Manuscripts
KEVIN ALLARDICE
NOVEL

Father Elegies
STELLA HAYES
POEMS

Slow Return
PAUL LIEBER
POEMS

Dreamer Paradise
DAVID QUIROZ
POEMS

How to Capture Carbon
CAMERON WALKER
STORIES

2023

God in Her Ruffled Dress
LISA B (LISA BERNSTEIN)
POEMS

Figures of Wood
MARÍA PÉREZ-TALAVERA
TRANSLATED BY PAUL FILEV
NOVEL

A Plea for Secular Gods: Elegies
BRYAN D. PRICE
POEMS

Nightfall Marginalia
SARAH MACLAY
POEMS

Romance World
TAMAR PERLA CANTWELL
STORIES

2022

No One Dies in Palmyra Ohio
HENRY ELIZABETH CHRISTOPHER
NOVEL

Us Clumsy Gods
ASH GOOD
POEMS

Skeletal Lights From Afar
FORREST ROTH
FLASH FICTION/PROSE POEMS

That Blue Trickster Time
AMY UYEMATSU
POEMS

2021

Pyre
MAUREEN ALSOP
POEMS

What Falls Away Is Always
KATHARINE HAAKE &
GAIL WRONSKY, EDITORS
ESSAYS

*The Eight Mile
Suspended Carnival*
REBECCA KUDER
NOVEL

Game
M.L. WILLIAMS
POEMS

2020

No, Don't
ELENA KARINA BYRNE
POEMS

One Strange Country
STELLA HAYES
POEMS

*Remembering Dismembrance:
A Critical Compendium*
DANIEL TAKESHI KRAUSE
NOVEL

Keeping Tahoe Blue
ANDREW TONKAVICH
STORIES

2019

Time Crunch
CATHY COLMAN
POEMS

Whole Night Through
L.I. HENLEY
POEMS

Echo Under Story
KATHERINE SILVER
NOVEL

Decoding Sparrows
MARIANO ZARO
POEMS

2018

Interrupted by the Sea
PAUL LIEBER
POEMS

The Headwaters of Nirvana
BILL MOHR
POEMS

2012

The Mermaid at the Americana Arms Motel
A.W. DEANNUNTIS
NOVEL

The Time of Quarantine
KATHARINE HAAKE
NOVEL

Frottage & Even As We Speak
MONA HOUGHTON
NOVELLAS

West of Eden:
A Life in 21ˢᵗ Century Los Angeles
CHUCK ROSENTHAL
MAGIC JOURNALISM

2010

Master Siger's Dream
A.W. DEANNUNTIS
NOVEL

Other Countries
RAMÓN GARCÍA
POEMS

A Giant Claw
GRONK
ESSAY BY GAIL WRONSKY
SPANISH TRANSLATION
BY ALICIA PARTNOY
ART

Coyote O'Donohughe's
History of Texas
CHUCK ROSENTHAL
NOVEL

So Quick Bright Things
GAIL WRONSKY
BILINGUAL, SPANISH TRANSLATION
BY ALICIA PARTNOY
POEMS

2009

Bling & Fringe
(The L.A. Poems)
MOLLY BENDALL &
GAIL WRONSKY
POEMS

April, May, and So On
FRANÇOIS CAMOIN
STORIES

One of Those Russian Novels
KEVIN CANTWELL
POEMS

The Origin of Stars
& Other Stories
KATHARINE HAAKE
STORIES

Lizard Dream
KAREN KEVORKIAN
POEMS

Are We Not There Yet?
Travels in Nepal,
North India, and Bhutan
CHUCK ROSENTHAL
MAGIC JOURNALISM

WHAT
BOOKS
PRESS

LOS ANGELES